Planes

Amy Shields

NATIONAL GEOGRAPHIC

Washington, D.C.

For Jenny, who hates to fly.

Text copyright © 2010 National Geographic Society

Published by the National Geographic Society, Washington, D.C. 20036. All rights reserved.
Reproduction in whole or in part without written permission of the publisher is strictly prohibited.

Library of Congress Cataloging-in-Publication Data

Shields, Amy.
Planes / by Amy Shields.
p. cm.
ISBN 978-1-4263-0712-6 (pbk. : alk. paper) -- ISBN 978-1-4263-0713-3 (library binding : alk. paper)
1. Airplanes--Juvenile literature. I. Title.
TL547.S5135 2010
629.133'34--dc22
2010011648

All photos of "Pilot Nic" by Becky Hale/National Geographic Staff; Cover, Robert Marien/ Corbis; 1, Kurt Rogers/ San
Francisco Chronicle/ Corbis; 2, Terrance Klassen/ Photolibrary; 4, Marcel Jolibois/ Photononstop/ Photolibrary; 6, Scott
Stulberg/ Corbis; 8, Georgios Alexandris/ Shutterstock; 10, Terry Mitchell/ US Air Force/ Department of Defense; 12, MSGT
Pat Nugent/ Department of Defense; 14, Robin Starr; 15, Staff Sgt. James Selesnick/ US Army; 17, Judson Brohmer/ USAF/
NASA; 18, AFP/ AFP/ Getty Images; 19 (top), Jenzinho/ Shutterstock; 19, Ian Waldie/ Bloomberg/ Getty Images; 21, Dwight
Smith/ Shutterstock; 22, 24 Mass Communication Specialist Seaman Brandon Morris/ US Navy; 25, Mass Communication
Specialist 2nd Class Milosz Reterski/ US Navy; 26, Gary Ell/ US Navy; 28, Fotosearch/ Getty Images; 31, Buyenlarge/ Getty
Images; 32 (top, left), Fotosearch/ Getty Images; 32 (top, right), Staff Sgt. James Selesnick/ US Army; 32 (middle, left), Mass
Communication Specialist Seaman Brandon Morris/ US Navy; 32 (middle, right), Dwight Smith/ Shutterstock; 32 (bottom,
left), Mass Communication Specialist 1st Class Heather Ewton/ US Navy; 32 (bottom, right), Judson Brohmer/ USAF/ NASA.

Printed in the United States of America
10/WOR/2

Table of Contents

Flying High

The pilot sits in the cockpit. We sit in the cabin. The cabin has TVs in the seats. It has bathrooms. It has a kitchen so we can have a snack. It is just like home, but 30,000 feet in the air.

Q Why did the elephant take so long to get to the airport?

A Because he had to pack his trunk.

Look out the window. From above, the Earth looks like a quilt of fields, forests, cities, and towns.

Sky Trucks

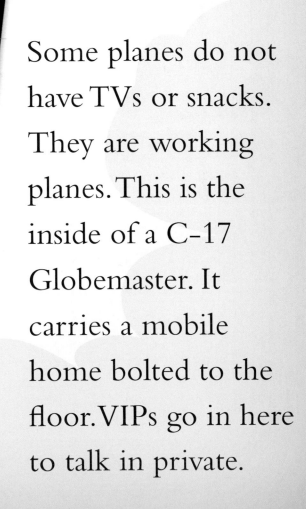

Some planes do not have TVs or snacks. They are working planes. This is the inside of a C-17 Globemaster. It carries a mobile home bolted to the floor. VIPs go in here to talk in private.

Some planes are built to carry stuff.
Big stuff. This is the Antonov 225.
It is the biggest plane ever made.
It is so big and heavy it needs 32
wheels to land.

Flying Bees

Bumble Bee I

The smallest plane used to be the Bumble Bee. It is 9½ feet long. Then came the Bumble Bee II. It was about a foot shorter.

There are even smaller planes, but they are not for people. This is a drone. It is flown by remote control.

Wing Words

DRONE: A plane driven by remote control

Fast and Fancy

The fastest plane is the SR-71 Blackbird. Only two people fit in this plane. It flies 3,418 miles an hour.

The SR-71 is a spy plane. Shhhhh!

Some planes are plain.
Some are painted.

The boomerang and the red plane come from Australia.

Wing Words

Propeller: An engine that turns blades to make the plane fly

Long ago some pilots painted their planes with scary faces. These planes are called Flying Tigers. They were flown in World War II.

City on the Sea

I'm here, you just can't see me!

Most planes leave the ground from a runway. But sometimes the runway is in the middle of the ocean. The U.S.S. *Enterprise* is an aircraft carrier. It carries 70 airplanes, 5,000 people, and enough cooks to make 15,000 meals a day!

The runway on the *Enterprise* is 20 stories above the ocean. Planes take off into the air from the deck. They go from 0 to 165 miles an hour in 2 seconds!

Landing is just as hard. Each plane has a tailhook. The hook catches on a wire to stop the plane. These pilots have nerves of steel.

These are jet airplanes.

Flying Gas Station

Wing Words

STEALTH: Secret, undercover

B-2 Stealth Bomber

Here is another pilot with nerves of steel. The little plane is a B-2 stealth bomber. The pilot is filling his gas tank while he is flying in the air!

Refueling tanker
say: ree-few-ling

Fill'er up!

The First

Orville Wright

Wilbur Wright

Anemometer
say: Ann-ee-MOM-ee-tur

Wing Words

ANEMOMETER: A tool for measuring wind speed

The Wright brothers were brave, too. They were the first to fly a plane. That was more than 100 years ago, but we still remember them. They were smart and unafraid, and they did it first. Hooray!

Take to the Sky

One hundred years before the Wright Brothers, someone else was dreaming of flying. But this balloon was never built, so no one ever flew it.

What are you dreaming about?

"La Minerve"
Vaisseau Aérien destiné aux Decouvertes
1803

ANEMOMETER: A tool for measuring wind speed

DRONE: A plane driven by remote control

JET: An engine that uses a stream of gases to make the plane fly

PROPELLER: An engine that turns blades to make the plane fly

STEALTH: Secret, undercover

VIP: Very Important Person